Fantastic Flying Fun With Science

DEDICATION

To Barbara,
my fantastic fun person

ACKNOWLEDGMENTS

We gratefully acknowledge the assistance of several people who provided information for *Fantastic Flying Fun*. Dan Roddick at Mattel Sports gave background information on the Frisbee® and other Wham-o products. Alan J. Adler, inventor of the Aerobie, shared information about his several inventions and about the aerodynamics of flying disks and rings. Mark Forti, who invented the X-zylo™ as a college student, sent information on flying cylinders. All of these people were gracious, patient, and a joy to talk to.

Each of the flying toy inventors sent samples for us to try. These toys provided our family with hours of fun, flinging together, as well as background for this book. Guys, I'm still having fun with the samples and hope you don't want them back. Thank you.

OTHER MCGRAW-HILL BOOKS BY ED SOBEY

Wacky Water Fun with Science

Just Plane Smart

Car Smarts: Activities for the Open Road

Wrapper Rockets and Trombone Straws: Science at Every Meal

FANTASTIC FLYING FUN WITH SCIENCE

Science you can fly, spin, launch, and ride

Ed Sobey, Ph.D.

Illustrated by Bill Burg

McGraw-Hill

New York   San Francisco   Washington, D.C.   Auckland   Bogotá
Caracas   Lisbon   London   Madrid   Mexico City   Milan
Montreal   New Delhi   San Juan   Singapore
Sydney   Tokyo   Toronto

McGraw-Hill

*A Division of The **McGraw-Hill** Companies*

1 2 3 4 5 6 7 8 9 0   DOC / DOC   0 9 8 7 6 5 4 3 2 1 0

ISBN   0-07-134800-X

Library of Congress Cataloging-in-Publication data applied for.

Printed and bound by R. R. Donnelley & Sons Company.

McGraw-Hill books are available at special quantity discounts to use as premiums and sales promotions. For more information, please write to the Director of Special Sales, McGraw-Hill, Two Penn Plaza, New York, NY 10121. Or contact your local book store.

Acquisitions editor: Griffin Hansbury
Senior editing supervisor: Jane Palmieri
Senior production supervisors: Clare B. Stanley and Charles Annis
Book design: Jaclyn J. Boone

Contents

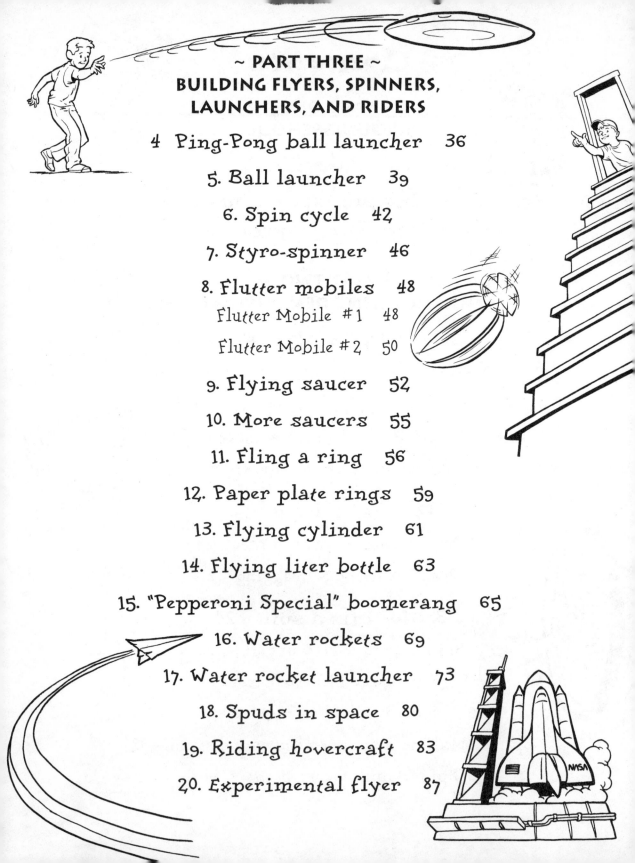

~ PART THREE ~
BUILDING FLYERS, SPINNERS, LAUNCHERS, AND RIDERS

~ PART ONE ~
GROUND SCHOOL

First takeoffs

Science, engineering, and technology are most fun when they are applied to making something you can fly, spin, launch, or ride. Skimming a homemade flying disk across a park demonstrates the design challenges of achieving level flight. Coaxing a boomerang to return consistently elevates curiosity about the physics of spin and lift. Folding a piece of paper into a screaming model paper airplane and lofting it out a second story window encourages thoughtful design to minimize drag.

We watch as some models stall and crash, some veer, some spin out of control, and some gently glide through the air taking our imaginations with them. Launching a water rocket one hundred feet awakens curiosity about air pressure and raises the inevitable question: "Can I get it higher?"

Such simple intrigues lead to building new models with new ideas, and developing an innate understanding of, and interest in, physics and engineering. Messing around with flying, spinning, launching, and riding things is a great way to learn.

Here is your opportunity to learn through experience the basics of lift, spin, drag, momentum transfer, and pressure. The best part is that you will be having a great time making fun devices that you can fly, spin, launch, and ride. Just follow the instructions and give a fling.

Of course, you can do more than follow our instructions: you can start there and go on to invent your own flyers, spinners, launchers, and riders. As you try new designs you will experience the fun of being an engineer and inventor. The big thrill will be testing your ideas and seeing them fly.

To get to that point you'll have endured a few failures and zany non-flights, but those experiences will make your successes even more enjoyable.

This process of developing an interest, conducting experiments, coming up with new ideas to overcome problems, and test-flying models led to the inventions of the airplane, the helicopter, the Aerobie, and the X-zylo. Now it's your turn to make a new flying, spinning, launching, or riding gizmo.

To help you navigate the science, we've provided navigational aids. These are road signs that tell you at a glance what the underlying science is. We've included some to show which projects would be great for science fairs. You can find these signs explained on the following pages.

Also, meet Wilbur the loon. A loon is equally at home in the air and on water. It must be fun to be a loon.

You can find navigational aids, along with Wilbur, in this book and in its companion, *Wacky Water Fun with Science* which has lots of building projects you can float, sink, squirt, and sail.

Your creativity coupled with your expanding understanding of aerodynamics and experience in flinging and flying can lead you to design all manner of things to fly, spin, launch, or ride. So "Wilburize" yourself and get ready to have fun!

Drag
What a drag!
Drag slows things down.

Lift
This sign tells you
the physics of lift apply.

Spin
Take a spin with activities
that have this sign.

Flyer
Let 'er fly.

Rider
Here's something you can ride.

Launcher
In the activities with this sign,
you can build devices to launch things.

Science Fair
Where you see a blue-ribbon
or microscope sign there is a
great science fair project for you.

What's Happening?
Sections with this sign give you the science behind the activity.

Converting fun experiments into science fair projects

So you're going to do a science fair project? Maybe that sounds like fun, or maybe it doesn't. Your first goal is making sure your project will be fun. Why? Because if your project turns into a chore, you're less likely to do a good job. You'll find other things to do instead of working on your project. If you pick a topic you really like, you'll work harder, learn more, and end up with a better science fair entry.

Many of the projects in this book lend themselves to science fair projects. Where we have seen obvious science fair possibilities, we've pointed them out. Look for one of these signs: Wilbur with a blue ribbon or Wilbur looking into a microscope.

To convert one of the projects in this book to a science fair topic, you will need to:

1. **Build and play with the flyer, spinner, launcher, or rider and ask yourself some questions about it** You might be intrigued to know how it works, or how high (or fast, or long) something can fly (or spin). You might be challenged to figure out a better way to fly it, spin it, launch it, or ride it. Whatever your questions are, write them in your science fair notebook. If you're having trouble coming up with questions, bring in some friends, members of your family, or your teacher. Show them what you've made and see if they can suggest topics for study.

2. Keep playing Playing around with stuff is how good science and inventing are done. Many great inventions arose when people played around with things that caught their attention. The microwave oven, the slinky, and Teflon are examples. The more you play with your device, the more neat stuff you'll notice and the more ideas you'll get. While you play, keep thinking about the questions you raised, and see what other questions come to your mind.

3. Pick a question You may have lots of questions, but you've got to focus on one for the science fair. You can work on the others later. What makes a good question? You will want to pick one that will let you do some experiments that give you numerical results.

As an example, you could compare how high a bottle rocket flies as you increase the pressure in the bottle (see project 16). You could record the air pressure in the bottle (from the gauge on a tire pump) and estimate how high the bottle flies.

To show your data, make a graph. On the horizontal axis show the pressure in pounds per square inch. Plot the height on the vertical axis.

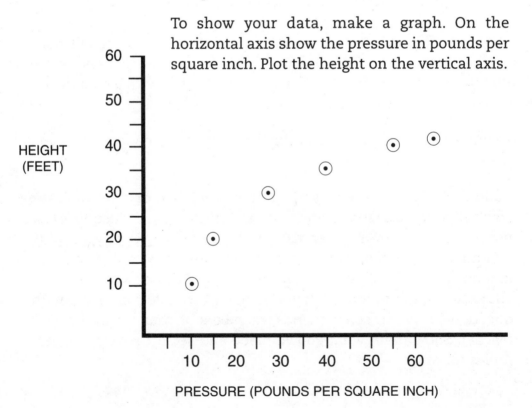

You want to choose a question that you will be able to answer in time for the science fair. Also, you will need to do some library research so you need a topic that you can find in books, research journals, magazines, on the INTERNET, or in videotapes. The librarian at your school or public library can help you find resources.

Of course you want to pick a question that's going to provide you with an experiment that will be fun to do.

4. Follow the guidelines   Make sure you understand how the science fair expects you to conduct your experiments and show your results.

5. Run your experiments   In the example of the water rocket project, you will want to repeat tests three or more times at each pressure so you can be sure your height measurement is precise. Then, with the averages of each height at each pressure, you could make a graph of the height versus the launching pressure.

6. Take some pictures   Take pictures of building and testing your device. They can make your presentation board look great.

7. Look at your data graph and see what story it tells   Does the height of the water rocket increase the same amount every time you increase the pressure five pounds? If it did, you could draw a straight line to connect all the data points. If a straight line wouldn't connect the points, what shape line would? If the points are scattered all over the graph, what does that tell you? See if you can figure out what story the graph tells, and if it makes sense with your understanding of the physics involved. If you can't figure it out, get some expert help at your school, a local high school, or a college. Keep asking questions until you know.

8. Write up the analysis and make your presentation   Reread the guidelines so you will create a presentation board and report that the science fair officials expect.

On the presentation board you will want to include photographs, the graphs of data, and the text and labels. If permitted, display the device you made in front of the board.

Did we leave anything out? Yes. Check those guidelines again. You may need to get your project approved before you start. Your school may want you to submit a research report before you start your experiments, but before that you need to do some experiments so you can decide what your project is going to be. So get started early so you have time to pick your project and do the library research on time.

Most of all, pick a project that you like and have fun. Science and inventing are supposed to be fun. Make sure your experience is.

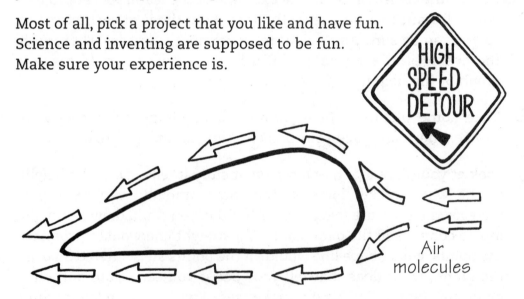

~ PART TWO ~
FANTASTIC FLYING DEMONSTRATIONS

Need a lift? 1

To fly, things need "lift." *Lift* is the upward force created when objects pass through air. Some things, like the wings on an airplane, provide lots of lift.

When you glance up to see an airplane in flight, remember that the only thing holding it up in the sky is the air moving over the top of the wing faster than it is underneath the wing. That movement of air provides lift. Frisbees need lift just as airplanes do. Interrupt the lift and the Frisbee flops to the ground.

Not everything that flies needs lift. A rocket uses its incredible engine power to thrust its way skyward, rather than using lift. The exhaust gases leaving the rear of the rocket push it forward. An artillery shell relies on the explosion inside the cannon to propel it. A blimp is a bag filled with lighter than air gases that let it float in air. But without a rocket engine, or lighter than air gas, flying things need lift to stay aloft.

Lift occurs when you can get air to move faster over the upper side of an object than underneath it. As air encounters an object, say a wing, some air travels over the wing and some goes under, but they both get to the trailing side of the wing at the same time. If the wing is the same shape on top and bottom, air moving above and below will travel the same distance and arrive at the trailing edge at the same time.

However, if the wing is curved to create lift, air has to travel farther along the upper surface than does air moving along the lower surface. The only way for it to take the same time to travel a longer distance is to speed up. And, faster moving air has lower air pressure. You can find that out in the next few experiments.

Lift 1: Wing it!

Show off your scientific abilities
in a restaurant, at home, or anywhere
with this breezy demonstration.

OVERVIEW Show the power of lift when you blow across
a strip of paper.

MATERIALS
- sheet of newspaper, napkin, or other paper
- your lips and lungs

PROCEDURE

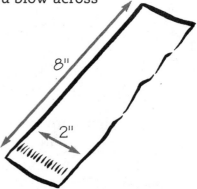

1. Tear a piece of paper about 2" wide and 8" long.

2. Hold one end between the thumb and forefinger of each hand, under your lower lip. The other end of the paper should dangle down in front of your chin.

3. Grab a breath and pucker up.

- What will happen when you blow across the top of the paper?

- Will the force of your breath push the paper down farther? After all, you will be pushing lots more air into the space above the paper than below it.

- Think about this, but don't hold your breath too long.

RESULTS
The paper flutters up.
It's flying!

WHAT'S HAPPENING?

The faster moving air across the top of the paper has lower air pressure than the still air underneath. The lower pressure above pulls the paper up.

What else?

◎ See how long a piece of paper you can blow up.

◎ Can you lift a strip as wide as an entire piece of the newspaper?

◎ Try lighter paper, like tissue paper, and heavier paper to see which works best. Can you get a hair dryer to lift a piece of paper?

DEMONSTRATION TIP

To demonstrate this effect in front of an audience, try these two variations:

❖ *Take two strips of paper and dangle each two inches apart, so one edge of each faces you. Blow between them. Do you expect the papers to move together (yes) or apart (no – get with the program!)?*

❖ *Tape the end of a string to a Ping-Pong ball so you can hang it by the string. Make a second one and dangle the pair in front of your puckered lips, and give a blast. Amazing, the balls move toward each other. But you knew they would.*

Lift 2: Flying wing

OVERVIEW   Demonstrate how a piece of cardboard can become a wing with lift.

MATERIALS
- string
- scissors
- masking tape
- hair dryer or shop vac

- cardboard from a cereal box (cardboard from a box of Fudgsicles works even better if you get to eat the Fudgsicles!)

PROCEDURE   **1.**   Find a safe place to stretch the string horizontally and tie it in place.

- Tie it as taut as you can. Make sure that it's in a place where no one will be walking.

2. Make the wing:

- Cut a 6" x 12" piece of cardboard.
- Wrap it around the string and tape the two (6" wide) ends together. Make sure the wing can swing easily on the string.
- The cardboard wing you just made should have a *symmetric* shape. That is, the top and bottom should have the same shape.

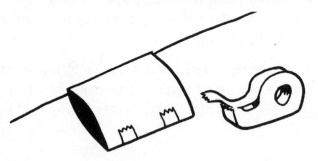

3. Test the wing:

- Using the low speed, blow on it with a hair dryer, or shop vac.
- Move the blower around: on top, in front, and underneath the wing to see how it responds.
- Is the blower powerful enough to give lift?

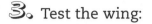

4. Change the shape of the wing:

- Bend the front of the wing up, and make the top bulge upward.
- Make the bottom flat and at least one inch shorter than it was before.

5. Test the new wing with the blower. Did the two wings respond to the moving air in the same way?

1"

RESULTS

The second model was a "Wilbur, I'm flying" success. By giving the wing a bulging curve on top, you increased the lift and up it flew.

IF IT DOESN'T WORK

Did you bulge the wing enough on top?

WHAT'S HAPPENING?

In airplanes the propeller or jet engine pulls or pushes the plane through the air and the passing air gives lift to the wings. Here you used a source of wind to generate lift on the wings. The low pressure resulting from high speed over the top of the wings pulled the wings up. The high speed resulted from air having to travel the longer surface (the bulging top) in the same time as did air traveling the shorter distance underneath.

What else?

◎ Try other shapes. Cut some more cardboard in the same dimensions, but bend it into more radical wing shapes. Then test them to see which flies best.

DEMONSTRATION TIP

❖ Try mounting three or more different wing models on the string at the same time. Then you can conduct side-by-side tests. Of course, this will require more cardboard, so you'll have to eat more Fudgsicles. But, you can do that for science.

FANTASTIC FLYING FACTS

A Boeing 747 generates 800,000 pounds of lift by air moving faster over the wing than under the wing. That upward force could raise 40 African elephants off the ground. But, who wants to have 40 elephants flying overhead?

Lift 3: Juggling a ball on a stream of air

OVERVIEW   You can balance a ball in midair, with lift.

MATERIALS   • Ping-Pong ball
• a straw that can bend
• your lips and lungs

PROCEDURE
1. Bend the straw into a ninety degree angle.
   • Hold it so you can blow into the longer end, with the shorter end pointing up.

2. Hold the Ping-Pong ball directly above the short end.

3. Take a deep breath (really deep) and blow through the straw as you release the Ping-Pong ball.

RESULTS   Wow! You kept the ball in midair!

IF IT DOESN'T WORK

Only a couple of things could go wrong. The most likely is that you need more lung power. If you've given it all you've got and the ball still doesn't fly, recruit a bigger set of lungs to try it. If that fails, check to make sure air is getting through the straw and that the Ping-Pong ball is in good (round, not dented) shape.

WHAT'S HAPPENING?

The air coming out of the straw is moving fastest in the center. Since faster moving air has lower air pressure, the pressure in the center is lowest and that sucks the ball to the center.

DEMONSTRATION TIP

❖ *Challenge your friends to balance the Ping-Pong ball in midair. When they give up, ask if they think you can do it. Then, bring out the straw and perform this demonstration.*

What else?

◎ Replace your lung power with a handheld hair blower. Turn on the blower, with the heat off, and point it upward. Place the ball in the air stream, and it will stay there.

◎ Try pointing the blower off to one side and seeing how far you can go before the ball falls out of the stream.

◎ Try two, or even three Ping-Pong balls at once!

Lift 4:
Wrap up the crowd

OVERVIEW   You'll get the crowd wrapped up in the science of lift.

MATERIALS
- a roll of bathroom tissue, 1-ply works best
- a spindle, or a dowel that fits inside the tissue tube (a wooden handle works well)
- a strong blower (a leaf blower, or shop vac that can blow)
- a seated audience waiting to be entertained

PROCEDURE

1. Load the bathroom tissue onto the spindle.
   - Hold it so the end of the roll is toward the audience and four or five sheets hang freely.

2. Switch the blower on and hold the nozzle a few inches above the roll.

3. Bring the nozzle down until the air stream catches the toilet paper and pulls it out into the audience.

17

RESULTS

Everyone is laughing!
You "Wilburized them" by covering them in toilet paper.

IF IT DOESN'T WORK

Is the blower strong enough to pull the toilet paper? Can the roll spin
freely on the spindle? If the paper blows apart, find a stronger brand.
If the audience didn't laugh, find a more appreciative audience.

WHAT'S HAPPENING?

The toilet paper got caught in the air stream, sucked in toward the
fastest moving air where the air pressure is lowest. It got sucked along
until the air stream weakened and then drifted down on the audience.

DEMONSTRATION TIP

❖ *Try this at home before you do it in front of an audience. It can be tricky
getting the best placement of the nozzle and the roll. You might recruit
an assistant to hold the spindle for you while you aim the nozzle. Consider
having a second roll ready in case the audience demands an encore. This is
a great demonstration!*

What a drag!

Drag is the resistance of air moving past a Frisbee, a 747, or a baseball in flight. To get a long flight, aeronautical designers minimize drag. When you ride your bike, you feel the drag, especially when you go fast. When you're zooming on your bike, how do you minimize the drag?

If you want to cycle fast, you scrunch down as small as possible to present less of your body to the slowing force of the air. Just as you minimize your body area to minimize the drag, designers of flying things minimize the area hitting the wind. In designing flying disks, they make the disk as thin as they can. The flatter the disk is, the less drag it will have, and the farther it will fly.

Compare the edges of throwing toys. They are designed to provide lift and to minimize drag. Can you predict which toy will travel farther based on how thin the edge is?

Drag is not some evil force we're always trying to overcome. Many times we want drag. That's why dragsters deploy parachutes at the end of a run — to slow them down. That's also why people who jump out of airplanes wear parachutes — so they won't land too fast.

For most flying things we make, we want to get the most lift possible and the least drag. But when you increase the lift, you also increase the drag. So designing flying things requires you to improve lift without adding too much drag.

Drag 1: One-meter drag race

OVERVIEW Two identical cards with pennies attached fall at different rates because one has much more drag than the other.

MATERIALS
- 2 index cards or other stiff cardboard
- 2 pennies
- glue
- meterstick

PROCEDURE **1.** Glue a penny on each card. On the first card, glue the penny in the center. On the second card, glue it along one of the short edges. Let the glue dry.

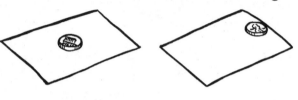

2. Hold both cards parallel to the ground at the same height, about one meter above the floor.

- Drop them simultaneously.

RESULTS The card with the penny in the middle will stay horizontal while the other card will fall vertically and fall much faster.

WHAT'S HAPPENING? Both cards have the same weight, but one presents a much larger surface area to the air due to the position of the penny, and falls slower. The smaller the area exposed, the less resistance there is. *Lower resistance allows higher speeds.*

DEMONSTRATION TIP

❖ *Try the same experiment with two identical flying disks. Drop one that is oriented vertically and the other horizontally. In designing flying things, or anything that moves quickly through air or water, drag matters.*

Drag 2: Lifting & dragging

OVERVIEW   You can measure the lift-to-drag ratio on paper airplanes and see what effect increasing the drag has.

MATERIALS
- 8 1/2" x 11" sheet of paper
- scissors
- clear tape, or masking tape
- yard stick, or tape measure

PROCEDURE

1. Make your favorite paper airplane, or build the model described in project 20.

2. Fly your model plane in a space large enough so it won't run into walls or objects.

3. Have someone measure the height of your hand when it's in position to release the plane.

4. Fling the plane and measure how far it flew.
- Fly the plane a few more times, measuring the distance each time.
- You want to launch it with the same force each time so it lands at about the same distance from you.

To calculate the average distance, add the distances the plane flew in three or more trials. Divide this by the number of trials. This number is the average distance. It should be shorter than the longest flight and longer than the shortest one. If it's not, check your mathematics.

$$\begin{array}{c} \text{Averaging} \\ \text{Distance} \\ \text{For Three} \\ \text{Throws} \end{array} \quad \begin{array}{r} 19' \\ 21' \\ + 17' \\ \hline 57' \end{array}$$

$$\frac{57'}{3} = 19'$$

$$\begin{array}{c} \text{Average} \\ \text{Distance} \end{array} = 19'$$

5. When you have the plane flying about the same distance each flight, calculate the average distance of three or more flights.

• Divide the average distance by the height of your arm. Make sure you use the same units of measurement; use inches for the height of your arm and inches for the distance thrown.

• The number you calculate is the *glide ratio*. If you know how to build other designs of paper airplanes, make them and calculate their glide ratio.

First Flight = 19'
2nd Flight 21'
3rd Flight = 17'
19 + 21 + 17 = 57
57 ÷ 3 = 19 Aver.

Height of
Sarah's arm 4.5'
19 ÷ 4.5 =
Glide Ratio

Compare the glide ratio of your plane to these. The glide ratio for a 747 means that it glides 15 feet for every foot it falls. An albatross, which is a large sea bird, can get 20 feet of gliding from only one foot of elevation. How does your paper plane compare?

albatross	20'
747	15'
robin	10'

MODIFY YOUR PLANE

- Cut a piece of paper 2" long x 1" wide. Fold the paper so 1 1/2" is on one side of the fold and 1/2" is on the other. Unfold the paper so it's flat.

- Tape the short side to the top of your plane, behind the balance point of the plane. Give it a test flight to see if it flies as far as it did before. It should.

- Raise the 1 1/2" flap you added to the top of the plane so it points straight up and refly it. You may have to bend the paper to keep it in this position.

- Measure the distance it flew and calculate the new glide ratio.

RESULTS

By adding the flap you increased the drag on the plane and reduced the glide ratio. The plane didn't fly as far.

SCIENCE FAIR

- You could add larger or smaller flaps to see how they effect the glide ratio.

- If you tested at least ten different size flaps you could graph the resulting glide ratio on one axis and the surface area of the flap on the other axis to get started on a Science Fair project.

3 Give this a spin

Some of the neatest things that fly have to spin so they can fly. Frisbees,® Aerobies,® flying cylinders, boomerangs, and helicopters all spin to fly. Spinning gives them lift and stability in flight, and makes them do strange things. Just pick up a flat rock or a piece of cardboard and fling it with spin to see the strange things that happen.

Experience tells us that when we throw something in a direction, it stays thrown in that direction. It doesn't do something silly like flying back to us. But that's what boomerangs do. A curve ball doesn't act quite as radically, but it does change direction after leaving a pitcher's hand. And, like a boomerang, it's the spinning that causes it to curve. When you fling a flat piece of cardboard, it turns over and dives to the ground. These all result from spin.

When a quarterback throws a long pass, he puts a spiral or spin on the ball. When a cannon shoots, it spins the shell to give it stability and greater range.

When you ride a bicycle, the spinning wheels provide stability which lets you sit balanced upright, as long as the bike is moving. Once the wheels stop, and the wheels no longer provide stability, the gyroscopes (wheels) quit working, and you had better be ready to catch yourself with your feet.

Can you ride without having your hands on the handle bars? How do you steer a bike without touching the handle bars? You lean to turn.

When you lean, the spinning
front wheel does something strange, it turns.
Fortunately for us bike riders, we live in a universe in which
spinning front wheels of bicycles turn in the same direction as we lean.

Boomerangs act very much like the front wheels of bikes. Like bike
wheels, boomerangs start out spinning vertically. And, like a no-hands
bike rider who is starting to turn, the boomerang responds to a lean by
turning toward the direction of the lean. It starts its path back to the
thrower. The lean, by the way, is produced by the boomerang having
more lift on its upper arm than its lower arm. We'll see how that
happens in project 15.

One thing to remember about spin is that the effects of a force show up
not where the force was applied, but a quarter of a circle away. You can
see that, along with how spinning effects stability, in the following
demonstrations.

Spin 1: Spin to stay upright

OVERVIEW You can trick a lot of people with this quick demonstration, especially if you don't tell them it's about spin.

MATERIALS
- quarter
- flying disk
- football

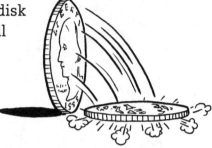

PROCEDURE

1. Try balancing the quarter, flying disk, or football on one end or edge.

- Can you get it to stay upright?
Try spinning it.

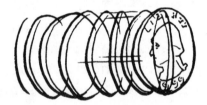

RESULTS With a good twist of the wrist, you were able to spin the disk, quarter, or football fast enough so it stayed upright for several seconds.

IF IT DOESN'T WORK

The football can be tricky. Start with it lying on it's side on the floor. Give it a mighty twist and it should spin up and wobble around on one end. Spinning it on a carpet floor covering is easier than on a slick floor.

WHAT'S HAPPENING?

Spinning gives stability. The spin prevents the quarter from falling over. As it starts to fall, gravity pulls the quarter, but the force on spinning objects acts a quarter circle or ninety degrees away. So the quarter pulls itself back up.

DEMONSTRATION TIP

❖ *Without saying anything about spin, challenge a friend to balance one of the three objects on a table. If they are able to balance the quarter or Frisbee on edge, or the football on its end, bump the table to disrupt their balance. Excuse yourself for hitting the table, and point out that they didn't get it to stay upright. When they protest that you cheated, tell them they can cheat while you do the balancing. For your turn, spin the object and let them shake the table. Even if they shake the table the spinning object will stay upright.*

Spin 2: How to blow your money

OVERVIEW By blowing on a spinning coin you can show why flat cardboard doesn't fly. The weirdness of spin moves it to one side.

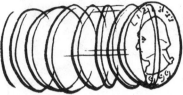

MATERIALS
- a coin
- flat table
- your lips and lungs

PROCEDURE **1.** Spin the coin on the table. Watch the coin to see which way its spinning. Is it spinning clockwise, when viewed from the top, or counterclockwise?

2. Now spin it again. With your lips at the same height above the table as the coin, try to blow it across the table.

RESULTS

You knew that it would move away from you, right? You expected it to go "down wind." But it also turned to one side. Did you expect that? If you spun it clockwise, your blowing moved it toward the right. Try it again, this time spinning it in the other direction. What direction will it move when you blow on it?

IF IT DOESN'T WORK

Make sure that you're blowing parallel to the surface of the table and that the coin is spinning long enough to see the effects.

WHAT'S HAPPENING?

When you apply a force to a spinning object, it moves in a direction a quarter circle or ninety degrees away from where the force was applied. You tried to blow it across the table, but it turned ninety degrees away from the direction you assumed it would go. This effect allows boomerangs to return and causes flying disks to veer to one side.

When you fling a piece of flat cardboard, the front edge catches the oncoming wind which pushes it upward. But, like blowing on the coin, the result shows up ninety degrees away. Instead of the front rising, a side rises sending the cardboard crashing to the ground. Fling it with your other hand, giving the cardboard opposite spin, and it crashes to the other side.

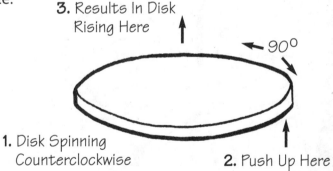

3. Results In Disk Rising Here

90°

1. Disk Spinning Counterclockwise

2. Push Up Here

DEMONSTRATION TIP

❖ *Make a par-one golf course with a sharp dogleg turn to each side and see if you can blow the coin into the hole using clockwise and counterclockwise spin.*

❖ *Make the fairway using cardboard and mark a target with a piece of masking tape. Can you get the coin to turn sharply enough to hit the target?*

Spin 3: Wheel science

OVERVIEW You can feel the weirdness of spin by holding a spinning bike wheel.

MATERIALS • 1 bicycle wheel

PROCEDURE 1. Take the front wheel off the bike.

2. Hold the ends of the axle in each hand, and have someone spin the wheel as fast as they can.

• Be careful not to have the spinning wheel brush up against you.

3. Once the wheel is spinning, raise your right hand and lower your left.

• Then, raise your left and lower your right hand.

4. Repeat this experiment, but this time without spinning the wheel. Can you feel the difference?

RESULTS

When the wheel was spinning and you raised your right hand, the wheel turned to the left. It did the opposite when you raised your left hand. This is just like making a turn on your bike when riding without your hands.

The faster the wheel spins, and the heavier the wheel is, the more dramatic the results will be.

When the wheel wasn't spinning, you didn't feel the wheel pull to either side when you raised one hand. Spinning caused the wheel to turn even when you didn't turn it.

WHAT'S HAPPENING?

You've become a bicycle! Or a boomerang! Leaning to your left while riding is the same as raising your right hand in the experiment. In each case, the spinning wheel turns toward the direction you're leaning. A boomerang behaves the same way.

DEMONSTRATION TIP

❖ *If you want to do this demonstration many times, you could make the wheel heavier. One way is to take the tire and inner tube off the wheel, and wrap a heavy material, like a roll of thick solder, around the wheel. Remount the tube and tire and inflate the tube.*

❖ *Sit in a chair that swivels easily with your feet off the floor. Hold the bike wheel as you did before and have someone give it a good spin. While holding the spinning bike wheel you can turn back and forth by raising and lowering your hands.*

Spin 4: Making a spin demonstration stand

OVERVIEW Make a rotating base so you can see and feel the effects of spin.

MATERIALS
- 18" square of $1/2$" plywood
- a heavy-duty swivel for a lazy Susan (from a hardware store)
- $3/8$" wood screws (to attach the swivel to the wood)
- screw driver
- drill

CONSTRUCTION

1. To make the rotating base:
- Get some adult help to cut the square of plywood.
- Center the swivel on one side of the wood.
- Drill starter holes for the screws.
- Screw the swivel to the wood.

2. Make sure it rotates freely. Try lubricating the bearings with some multipurpose oil if it doesn't swivel easily.

PROCEDURE

1. When using the demonstration stand, have someone help you get on and off as it can be tricky keeping your balance.

2. It's safer to sit than stand. Cross your legs and center yourself on the plywood.

3. You can use this spin demonstration stand for "Spin 3" or to show the conservation of angular momentum in "Spin 5."

4. When using a spinning bike wheel, have someone spin the bike wheel and hand it to you.

Spin 5: Spin me up, Scotty

OVERVIEW   Spin around faster on the spin demonstration stand to demonstrate the conservation of angular momentum.

MATERIALS
- the spin demonstration stand from "Spin 4," or a swivel chair that spins easily
- some weights – five pound dumbbells or two 2-liter bottles filled with water
- a friend who likes to spin

PROCEDURE   **1.** Sit centered on the demonstration stand or swivel chair.

- Making sure your feet, legs, and everything else are off the floor and on the turning surface.

- Take a trial spin, without the weights, so you can reposition yourself in the center if you need to.

2. Grasp one weight in each hand, with your arms fully extended to the sides.

3. Have your friend gently spin you. Make sure you are spinning freely without anything dragging on the floor.

4. As soon as you are spinning, pull your arms in toward your chest. Bring your arms in to speed up, and then out again to slow down. Then in again to speed up once more.

RESULTS

Wow! You were spinning slowly until you brought your arms in. Then, wham!, you were spinning like the spin cycle of a washing machine. You have to feel it to believe it.

WHAT'S HAPPENING?

Spinning things keep the same angular momentum. *Angular momentum* is the rate of spinning multiplied by "moment of inertia." The moment of inertia depends on the weight of the stuff that's spinning and its distance from the center. The farther the weight is from the center of the spin, the higher your moment of inertia.

Your friend gave you angular momentum when she spun you. You had a distribution of weight that included the two dumbells. Without another force coming into play, the angular momentum will stay the same. When you pulled in your arms, bringing the weights closer to the center of spin, the distribution of weight changed and you reduced your moment of inertia. The only way for angular momentum to stay the same (since you decreased the moment of inertia) is for spin to increase.

DEMONSTRATION TIP

❖ *Watching someone else do this experiment is fun, but feeling the rotation rate increase for yourself can be wild!*

~ PART THREE ~
BUILDING FLYERS, SPINNERS, LAUNCHERS, AND RIDERS

4 Ping-Pong ball launcher

OVERVIEW Launch Ping-Pong balls with a stream of air. See how fast-moving air sucks balls into the air stream, and then launches them across the room.

MATERIALS
- hair dryer, shop vaccuum, or electric leaf blower
- 1' length x 1½" diameter PVC pipe
- 4' length x 1½" diameter PVC pipe
- PVC "T" fitting for 1½" pipe
- box of Ping-Pong balls
- sandpaper

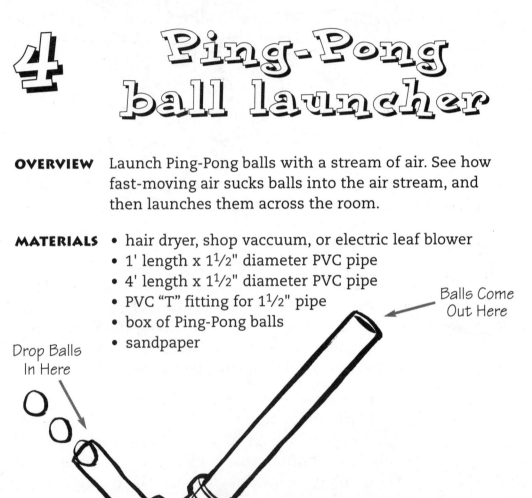

Drop Balls In Here

Balls Come Out Here

CONSTRUCTION

1. Use the sandpaper to smooth the ends of the PVC pipe so you won't cut yourself.

2. Fit the foot-long piece of PVC pipe into the middle leg of the "T."

3. Insert the blower into one of the other two ends of the "T." Position it so the stream of air leaves the blower at the center of the "T," without blocking Ping-Pong balls coming from the middle leg.

4. Adjust the placement until you feel suction on the end of the PVC pipe in the middle leg when you turn on the blower.

5. Use the 4' length of PVC pipe for the launch tube by jamming it into the remaining end of the "T."

ACTION Launch only in safe areas. Have the Ping-Pong balls ready. Point the launch tube upward, away from people and things. Turn on the blower and let the suction on the middle leg of the "T" pull in Ping-Pong balls.

WHOMP!

WHAT'S HAPPENING? When it is confined inside the tube, the stream of air accelerates the Ping-Pong balls. Try holding a Ping-Pong ball above the blower without the launch tube. You can get the ball to balance in midair, but not to launch across the yard.

What else?

◎ If using this in front of an audience, have a box of Ping-Pong balls ready. Ask a friend to assist you by holding the launch tube while you rapidly load it. You'll bombard the crowd, but your demonstration won't bomb.

SCIENCE FAIR

There are several potential projects here.

- Investigate what effect the length of the launching pipe has on the distance balls are thrown.

- Would heavier balls travel farther? Launch only in safe areas, and be careful not to do damage with a golf ball or other dense ball.

- Compare launch distances in warm air to distances in cold air. Which do you suppose would give longer flights?

- Make a graph to compare the distance the ball travels and the angle the launch tube makes with the vertical. What angle do you think will give the farthest, and highest, launch?

Ball launcher

OVERVIEW Launch a tennis ball thirty feet into the air using a momentum-transfer launcher made of a basketball and a tin can.

MATERIALS
- basketball
- 2 tennis balls
- tin can
- a variety of lighter balls
- duct tape

CONSTRUCTION

1. Use a can opener to remove both ends of the tin can. Be careful not to cut yourself.

2. Tape the can to the basketball so one end is resting on the ball.

ACTION

1. **Caution:** You need to go outside, unless you're in a room with very high ceilings.

2. Hold the basketball at eye level, with the can facing up and drop the ball. See how high it bounces.

3. Now, load one tennis ball in the can (pointing up), and repeat step 2. See how high the tennis ball flies.

4. Repeat step 3, but this time watch how high the basketball rebounds. Did it bounce as high as it did without the tennis ball in the launcher?

5. Try launching two tennis balls at once. Try other lighter balls.

- Find out what combination gives the highest launch.
- Remember to watch how high the basketball bounces as you add more balls to the launcher.

RESULTS You were able to launch the tennis ball twenty to thirty feet by dropping the launcher only five feet.

WHAT'S HAPPENING? As the basketball hits the ground, some of its momentum (*mass x velocity*) is transferred to the lighter tennis ball, launching the tennis ball high.

Because the basketball is heavier, it had more momentum than the tennis ball. When the basketball hit the ground and collided with the tennis ball, some of its momentum was transferred to the tennis ball. With more momentum, the tennis ball went high. With less momentum, the basketball didn't rebound as high.

Momentum is mass multiplied by velocity. In football, a 200-pound lineman has twice the momentum a 100-pound end has, if they are running at the same speed. A 200-pound lineman running twice as fast as another 200-pound lineman has twice the momentum. We recommend you experiment with the tennis ball launcher and not the 200-pound lineman.

DEMONSTRATION TIP *Surprisingly few people have seen this, and most are amazed at how high the lighter balls fly. Make sure the basketball is inflated to the recommended air pressure to get the best rebound. Make sure you don't do this below anything breakable, like light bulbs.*

SCIENCE
FAIR

- This could be the start for a great Science Fair project. You could have fun, collect numerical data, and have a demonstration to show.

- A basic project would be to study the momentum transfer by measuring the rebound height of the basketball compared to the dropping height.

- You could drop the basketball from various heights and measure how high it rebounds both with and without a tennis ball in the launcher.

- Also, measure how high the tennis ball flies. The tricky part will be ensuring that the launcher always faces upward, and accurately measuring the heights.

- Make a graph of the drop height compared to the height of the tennis ball and another graph comparing drop height of the basketball to its rebound height.

Spin cycle

OVERVIEW   Make a top and see how long you can keep it spinning.

MATERIALS
- 1/4" dowel, at least 8" long
- saw
- paper plates
- nail
- pencil sharpener
- tin snips or wire cutter
- glue

CONSTRUCTION

1. Make an 8" long spindle from the 1/4" dowel.

   - Use the tin snips or wire cutter to cut part way through dowel. Then snap the dowel apart.

2. Sharpen one end of the spindle with a pencil sharpener.

3. Find the center balance point of a paper plate. The easiest way to find the center is to balance the plate on the flat end of the spindle.

   - When you have located the balance point, poke a hole through the center with a nail.

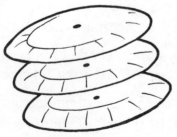

4. Stack two or more paper plates centered on top of the first plate.

   - Position the plates so that the center holes are aligned.

5. Firmly secure the spindle in place with some glue. While the glue is drying, hold the spindle vertically with the disk lying horizontally.

ACTION With the sharp end of the spindle on the floor or table, hold the spindle between the palms of your hands and slide them in opposite directions.

RESULTS With a hearty spin the top will stay upright and spinning for several seconds.

IF IT DIDN'T WORK Make sure the spindle is firmly attached to the plate. If you get it spinning, but it stops too soon, you may need more weight, or you may not have the spindle centered.

WHAT'S HAPPENING? The top keeps spinning until friction slows it down. As long as it's spinning, it exhibits the "gyroscopic effect." You can balance the top on the end of its spindle, but only while it's spinning.

What else?

◎ Try adding some pennies, or washers, as weights to the outside of the plate.

Scribbling top

Use a pencil for the spindle. Spin it on top of a large piece of paper to see what patterns show up.

Trick your eyes top

Use a black marker, or paint, to color one half of the top black, leaving the other half white. Then spin the top. Do you see color? When the top stops spinning, you'll see only black and white, but while it spins you may see color. You have tricked your eyes. Try painting colorful patterns on the top to see what it looks like when you spin it.

Top launcher

Spin longer with a top launcher. Use a piece of wood 6" long and 4" wide by 3/4" thick. One inch in from an end, nail two brads or small nails; mark a spot 1/2" from the top and 1/2" from the bottom. Drive in each brad so about half is sticking out. After they're in, give each a tap with the hammer to bend them toward the near end.

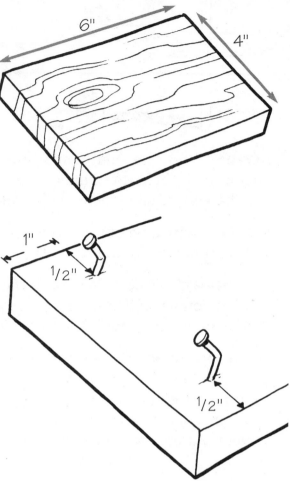

Now wind string around the spindle of a top about ten turns. Hold the spindle vertically so it rests against the two nails. You can hold the spindle with your index and middle fingers and the block of wood with your thumb and pinkie.

If this is too hard to hold, ask someone to hold the top and launcher while you hold the string. Pull the string to spin the top. As you do, let go of the spindle so the spinning top falls to the floor and continues to spin.

SCIENCE FAIR

- Investigating tops could make a fun project. What makes a top spin longer?

- Could you figure out several things that might change how long a top can spin?

- You could change one of them at a time and keep records of how long the different tops spun. You might start by trying to spin a spindle without a plate.

- You could try adding more and more plates to see if the added weight gives longer or shorter spins. Or, you could add weights to either the outer edge, middle, or center of the top.

- You will want to take at least three trials (time measurements) with each model and average the results. Figure out a good way to show your data on a piece of graph paper. And, keep spinning.

7 Styro-spinner

OVERVIEW Here's an easy to make helicopter that spins to slow its fall.

MATERIALS
- styrene meat tray
- scissors
- large paper clip
- styro-spinner pattern

CONSTRUCTION

1. Use the pattern below to cut out the styro-spinner shape from the styrene meat tray.

• You can try a variety of sizes and shapes, but start with the one shown here.

2. Add the paper clip to the straight-edge end.

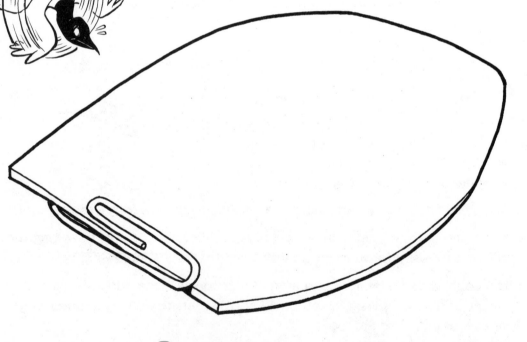

3. Stand on your back porch, steps, or some other high place and launch it.

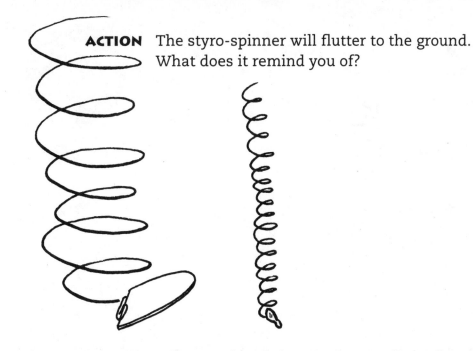

ACTION The styro-spinner will flutter to the ground. What does it remind you of?

RESULTS The spinner flutters the same way as a maple seed pod. You might look for a maple seed pod and drop it alongside the spinner. Which travels slower?

IF IT DOESN'T WORK Give it a twist. Bend the styrene.

WHAT'S HAPPENING?
As the spinner falls air rushes past it causing it to rotate, which gives stability to the flight (fall). Air hitting the lower side slows the fall. Helicopters can lose engine power and fall safely to the ground just like your styro-spinner did as the air passing the rotors spins them and slows the descent.

What else?

◎ How big can you make a styro-spinner and have it work? If you make very large spinners, add enough weight so the narrow end falls first. If it doesn't flutter, try bending the two edges inward.

8  **Flutter mobiles**

OVERVIEW You can make a helicopter-like flyer out of paper. It spins as it falls through the air.

MATERIALS
- 8½" x 11" sheet of paper
- flutter pattern
- scissors
- tape
- paper clips

Flutter Mobile #1

CONSTRUCTION

1. Cut a strip 1" wide and 8½" long from the sheet of paper.

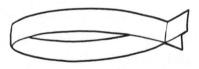

← Cut Notch   Cut Notch →

2. Measure 1" from each end of the strip, and cut a ½" notch on opposite sides of the flutter mobile.

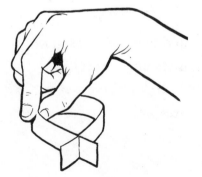

3. Bend the strip over on itself so you can connect the two ends together by matching up the two notches and sliding them together.

ACTION

Hold the Flutter Mobile #1 by one of the sides and drop it from the top of a set of stairs.

RESULTS

It will flutter nicely, spinning and slowly falling to the ground.

Flutter Mobile #2

CONSTRUCTION

1. Trace or copy the pattern shown here onto a piece of paper.

2. Cut out the shape.
• Cut on the lines that are solid and fold on the lines that are dashed.

3. Bend the wings in opposite directions, perpendicular to the rest of the mobile.

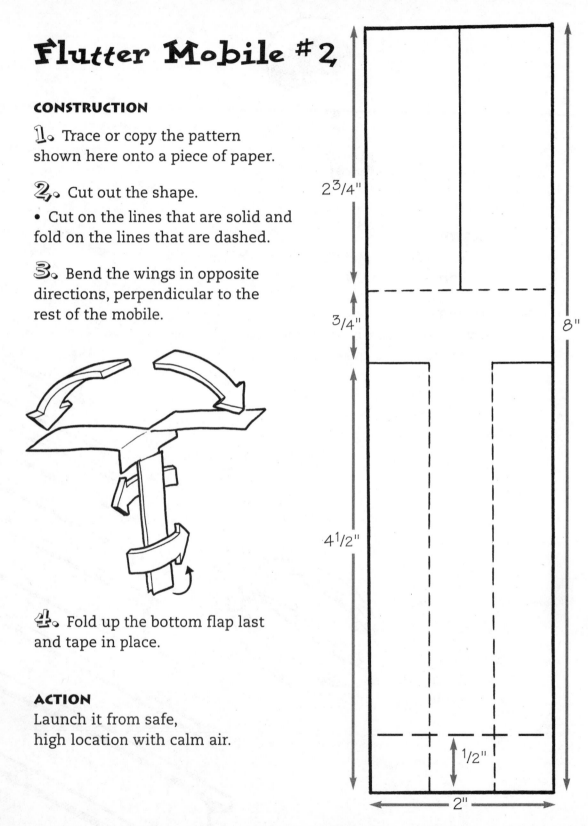

4. Fold up the bottom flap last and tape in place.

ACTION
Launch it from safe, high location with calm air.

RESULTS It will auto-rotate to the ground.

WHAT'S HAPPENING? Auto-rotating is the spinning that occurs when air passing the rotors causes them to spin. The spinning gives lift thus slowing the fall.

What else?

◎ Try adding some weight in the form of a paper clip.
Does that improve the flight characteristics? Would two be even better?

◎ Can you make a larger Flutter Mobile?
Use a copier that enlarges so you can try bigger and smaller versions of the pattern shown. See what size works best.

◎ Would heavier paper work better? Try using construction paper, or two sheets of regular paper cut, folded, and taped together.

9 Flying saucer

OVERVIEW   Make a flying disk. Better yet, make lots of them.
You can explore how spinning gives great flights.

MATERIALS
- corrugated cardboard
  (at least 10" square)
- compass for drawing circles
- scissors

CONSTRUCTION

1. Cut a 10" diameter circle
out of a piece of corrugated cardboard.
Use a compass so you can draw the circle precisely.

- Poke the sharp point of the compass
into the center of the cardboard and,
with a 5" radius, draw a circle.

- Cut it out with scissors.

ACTION

You need to be outside or in
a gymnasium to test fly your disk.
With a flip of your wrist, give it a fling.
What happens?

RESULTS

If you toss it with your right hand, the right side rises and it flips over
to the left. Try tossing it with your left hand. It will crash to the right.
We need to modify the saucer to make it fly better.

WHAT'S HAPPENING?

The spinning disk had unbalanced forces
acting on it and, like all spinning things, the
resulting action shows up a quarter circle
away from the cause. The unbalanced force
was air pushing up the front of the disk as it
flew forward. The resulting action was that
one side, depending on the direction of the
spin, rose causing the disk to crash. If you flew
it right-handed, it crashed to the left.

FANTASTIC FLYING FACTS

Over 90% of the people in the
United States have flown a flying disk.
If you could invent an improved flying disk,
you could become a bazillionaire.

With your hardest throw,
how long could you keep a flying disk in the air?
The world record is 16.72 seconds. See if you can beat it.

If you flung a flying disk for 24 hours, how far would it have gone?
The 24-hour distance record is 367 miles.

The Frisbee gains lift in three ways. When you fling it,
you give it a slight upward angle and air hitting the underside
pushes it upward. The Frisbee also acts like a wing and air
passing over and under the wing give it lift (see Lift 1).
The spin of the Frisbee also generates lift. But don't ask us how.

How far could you fling a flying disk?
The outdoor record for men is 656 feet,
and for women the record is 447 feet.

SCIENCE FAIR

- Compare the flight times and maximum distances of different models of flying disks.

- You could compare ones you buy and ones you make. Measure the thickness and diameter of each disk.

- If you have access to a postal scale you could also weigh each. See if heavy ones fly farther or models with the thinnest disk do.

More saucers 10

OVERVIEW   You can make great flying disks with paper plates. Spinning plates work like Frisbees do.

MATERIALS
- paper plates
- glue
- 6 pennies or washers

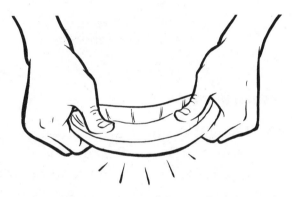

CONSTRUCTION

1. Turn one of the plates inside out.

2. Place a second plate on a table, upside down.

3. Mount the inside-out plate on top of the second plate and glue them together.

4. Glue six evenly spaced pennies around the top edge. Give it a fling. This is the six-cent flyer.

RESULTS   This disk should fly far.

What else?

◎ Try building disks with different numbers of paper plates and weights.

11 Fling a ring

OVERVIEW Make a flying ring and see how it flies compared to a flying disk.

MATERIALS
- 2 pieces of corrugated cardboard (each at least 10" square)
- compass for drawing circles
- scissors
- glue
- kitchen spoon
- blunt kitchen knife

CONSTRUCTION

1. Using the compass, draw two concentric circles on the cardboard (two circles with the same center point).

- Give the outer circle a 10" diameter and the inner circle a 6" diameter.

2. Use scissors to cut out the ring.

3. Give it a fling.

TUNE IT You can improve the flight characteristics by tuning the ring. Bend down the outer edge of your ring by holding a section of the edge just over the end of a table and press on the edge with a spoon. Rotate the ring and repeat, pressing down to get an even angle all the way around. Fling it again. Did tuning it improve the flight?

REENGINEERING You can improve the ring by adding a second ring.

- Draw and cut out a second ring with an outer diameter of $8^1/2$" and an inner diameter of 6".

- Glue the two rings together so the center openings align.

- Once the glue dries, give this a try. With a little tuning, you will have a great indoor flying ring.

FANTASTIC FLYING FACTS

We don't know if George Washington tossed a dollar across the Potomac River, but we do know that Scott Zimmerman flung an Aerobie across Niagara Falls.

CHECK OUT AN AEROBIE®

Look at the odd shape of the upper surface — from the outside of the ring to the inside. The inventor, Alan Adler, came up with the design to overcome the tendency of spinning flying things to veer to one side. You could add a similar "lip" to your flying ring. Alan suggests:

• Use a blunt kitchen knife to separate the cardboard at the outer edge. Cut between the upper and lower surface of the ring. (Be careful using a knife as it could slip and separate some skin instead of cardboard.)

• Bend the top up slightly (tune it) at an even angle all the way around.

Paper plate rings 12

OVERVIEW Build spinning flying rings out of paper plates.

MATERIALS • paper plates (or recyclable plastic plates)
  • scissors
  • glue

CONSTRUCTION

To make a ring, cut the center out of a paper plate using the line marking the bottom of the plate as a guide.

• Try flinging one.

• Try the two options below to make it fly like a champion.

Option 1 • Place one ring on a table with the bottom side down.

• Take an uncut plate and place it upside down on top of the first ring.

• Glue the edges of the two plates together.

• Decorate appropriately. It looks like a flying saucer.

Option 2 • Follow the directions for Option 1, and use two rings glued together, and mount an uncut plate on top.

ACTION Fling these with the ring on the bottom and the whole plate(s) on top. Compare the flight characteristics between the flying rings and disks that you have made so far. Which flies best? Which flies farthest? Can you make them fly farther?

FANTASTIC FLYING FACTS

In 1986 Scott Zimmerman threw an Aerobie farther than anyone had ever thrown any object. Scott's throw covered 1,257 feet.

Flying cylinder

OVERVIEW Make a flying cylinder out of paper and check out how well a cylinder can fly.

MATERIALS
- 8 1/2" x 11" sheet of paper
- clear tape or a paper stapler
- quarter or blunt kitchen knife

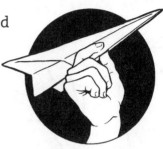

CONSTRUCTION

1. Draw a line parallel to the long edge of the paper, about 1/2" in from edge.

- Lightly score this line with a quarter to make it easier to fold.

2. Fold the paper over the line.

- Continue folding 1/2" strips until 2 1/2" of unfolded paper remains.

3. Make a cylinder.

- With the folds on the outside, roll the paper lengthwise and tuck one end inside the other.

- Tape or staple the two ends together.

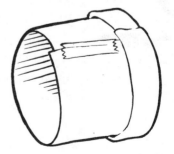

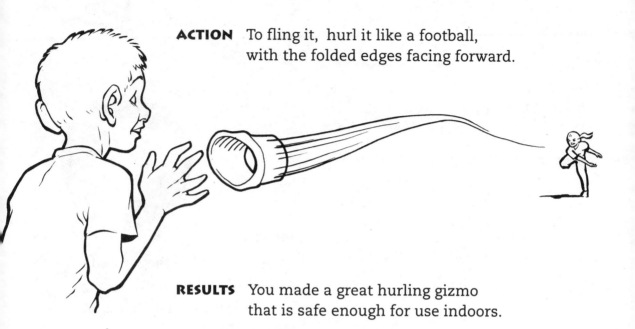

ACTION To fling it, hurl it like a football, with the folded edges facing forward.

RESULTS You made a great hurling gizmo that is safe enough for use indoors.

What else?

◎ Try other sizes of paper to see what else works well.

FANTASTIC FLYING FACTS

You can imagine a college student folding paper airplanes and flinging them across his dorm room. It's a mindless way to relax. But for Mark Forti, it stimulated an idea. He started hurling paper cylinders across his dorm room at Baylor University and that led him to invent the X-zylo, plastic flying cylinder you can buy in toy stores.

Flying liter bottle 14

OVERVIEW This soda bottle model is easy to make and flies well.

MATERIALS
- one-liter plastic soda bottle
- marker
- scissors
- glue or tape
- electrical power cord from a discarded appliance or from an appliance repair store
- wire cutters
- paper clips

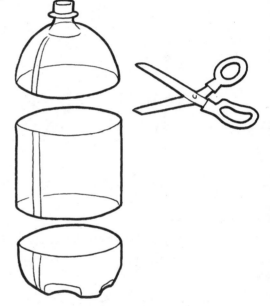

CONSTRUCTION

1. Make a cylinder 3 to 4 inches long:

- With a marker, draw a straight guide line around the top and around the bottom of the soda bottle.

- Use the scissors to cut off the top and bottom of the bottle.

2. Put a bead of glue around the edge of the cylinder and wrap the electrical power cord around it.

- Paper clip the cord in place until the glue is completely dry.

- Then remove the paper clips.

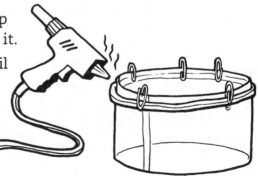

ACTION

Fling this flyer by tossing it like a football, with the cord-weighted end facing forward. Roll it off your finger tips to give it a spiral as you throw it.

WHAT'S HAPPENING?

No one knows why a cylinder flies so well. Spinning gives it stability and air passing through the cylinder gives it lift. Try experimenting to see if you can learn more about how it flies so well.

FANTASTIC FLYING FACTS

How far could you fling your gizmo?
A commercially made flying cylinder, the X-zylo,
flew 655 feet. There are only a few devices,
like the Aerobie, that have flown farther.

"Pepperoni Special" boomerang

OVERVIEW Here are boomerangs that are safe to fling indoors and return to you every time.

MATERIALS
- pattern
- pizza box
- scissors
- pencil
- an enlarging copier

CONSTRUCTION

1. Order a large pepperoni pizza.

2. While waiting for the pizza to arrive, make a photocopy enlargement of the triblader pattern (found on the next page) so that the distance between dashed lines measures 6".
- Cut out the shape.

3. As soon as the pizza arrives, eat the pizza and save the box. Trace the outline of the tribladed boomerang on the inside of the lid.

4. Cut the shape out of the pizza box lid.
- Call your boomerang the "Pepperoni Special."

5. Place the triblader on a flat surface and bend each of the arms upward just enough so they stay slightly bent.
- Mark the side facing up with the letters "PS" for Pepperoni Special.

6"

FLINGING

Now you're ready to whirl. Hold the boomerang in a vertical orientation between your thumb and forefinger of either hand with the "PS" facing inward. With a flick of your wrist, release the boomerang. You may need to take a few practice flings to get the correct wrist action. The "PS" will fly in a circle with a diameter of five or six feet and will return to you.

RESULT

With a bit of practice you'll be able to catch your boomerang every toss.

WHAT'S HAPPENING?

The spinning arms create an unbalanced force, lift, which causes the boomerang to turn. As it turns, it lays over so it's spinning horizontally. From this, the highest point of its trajectory, the boomerang slowly falls and rotates back to you.

What else?

◎ What happens when *two* of the arms are bent as described
on page 65 and one is bent in *the* opposite direction?
Find *the* optimum angle of bend.
Does a slight twist improve *the* flying?

◎ Take your flying triblader *to* an enlarging copier and make
a copy at 150%. Use *this* pattern *to* make another cardboard triblader.
How big can you make *this* model and *still* have it return?

◎ Try cutting out a second triblader, identical *to* the first one
you made, and glue it on top of your first one. Align *the* arms so they
are evenly spaced, giving you a six-blader. See if you can get *this*
to return. You will need *to* bend *the* arms, and you might want
to trim *the* arms. Does i*t* fly as well as the original triblader?

Water rockets

OVERVIEW Make a rocket that shoots across the park. You provide the energy by pumping up air pressure in the rocket.

MATERIALS
- a two-liter plastic bottle
- a one-hole rubber stopper or a cork
- bicycle tire pump
- inflation needle, used for filling basketballs
- nail
- glue or Shoe Goo® (sold at athletic stores)
- water
- a board, at least 12" square

CONSTRUCTION

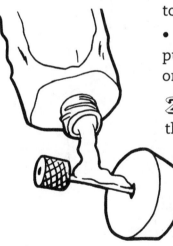

1. The challenge is getting the inflation needle to stick through the stopper or cork.

• You will connect the inflation needle to the pump so you want the connection on the outside or larger side of the stopper.

2. If the hole in the stopper is too large, fill the hole with glue or, even better, Shoe Goo®.

> • This is tricky: you cannot pour the glue or Goo into the hole and then insert the needle; the sticky material will clog the opening in the needle.

> • Instead, glob the stuff on the shaft of the needle, keeping it away from the opening at the end.

3. Insert the needle into the hole.

• If you are using a cork, use a small nail to make a hole through the center of the cork, and then insert the needle through the hole.

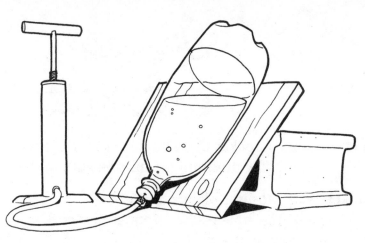

LAUNCHING

Set up the launch ramp, the board, so it angles upward about 45 degrees. Make sure that it is pointed toward an open area where no one and nothing could be hurt.

Fill the bottle half way with water. Water has to cover the stopper and needle. Attach the needle to the pump and place the bottle, bottom-side up, on the launch pad. Pump up the pressure until the bottle takes off.

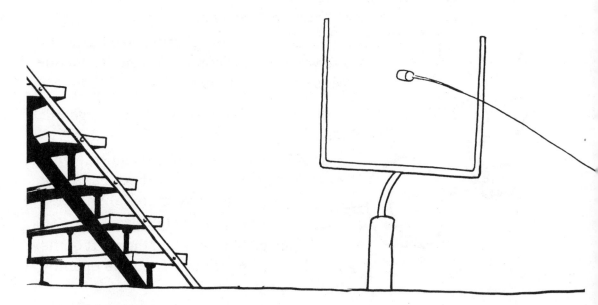

CAUTION Make sure the bottle is directed so no person, animal, or anything else is in the flight path. Don't wedge the stopper or cork so far into the bottle that it won't come out. The bottle should fly off after just a few strokes of the pump. If it requires lots more pumping, the cork may be in too tightly. At high enough pressures the plastic bottle will explode sending plastic shards everywhere. This is a bad thing.

RESULTS You can launch a bottle rocket 50 feet into the air.

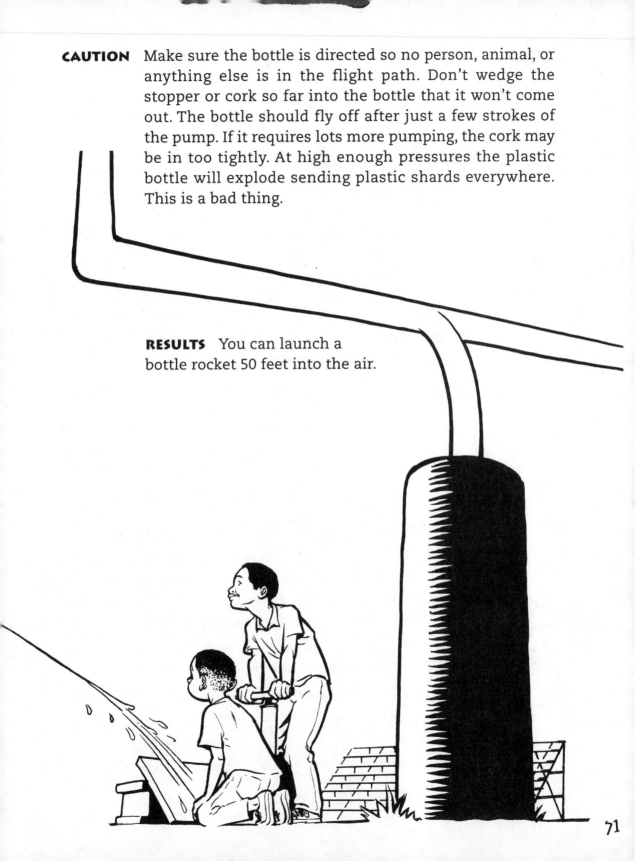

WHAT'S HAPPENING?

The pressure inside the bottle forces the water and air out the opening, which propels the bottle in the opposite direction.

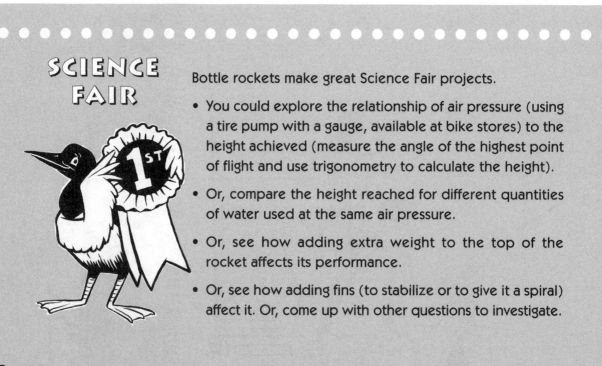

SCIENCE FAIR

Bottle rockets make great Science Fair projects.

- You could explore the relationship of air pressure (using a tire pump with a gauge, available at bike stores) to the height achieved (measure the angle of the highest point of flight and use trigonometry to calculate the height).

- Or, compare the height reached for different quantities of water used at the same air pressure.

- Or, see how adding extra weight to the top of the rocket affects its performance.

- Or, see how adding fins (to stabilize or to give it a spiral) affect it. Or, come up with other questions to investigate.

Water rocket launcher 17

OVERVIEW Build a launcher for water rockets.

MATERIALS

- a sheet of 3/4" plywood for the base
- a one-hole rubber stopper
- 1/2" PVC elbow (male)
- 3 screw eyes with 3/4" openings
- 3/4" diameter dowel, 1' long
- 6' long light rope or clothesline
- 27" long steel bar, 1/8" thick x 3/4" wide
- tire valve
- 5/8" rubber hose, 5' long
- 3 1/4" bolts, 2 1/2" long
- 2 1/2" hose clamps
- 3 wing nuts, 1/4"
- 3 3/4" springs
- nails 1 1/2" long
- wood glue
- epoxy
- neoprene washer or piece of wet suit, 4" diameter x 1/8" thick

TOOLS

- drill with bits
- wood saw
- bicycle air pump, with gauge
- safety goggles

CONSTRUCTION

This is going to take an afternoon, but you will be delighted you made it.

• Wear safety goggles for eye protection during construction.

1. Build a 2-foot square base.

• Using a wood saw, cut an identical 2-foot square top and bottom out of the plywood.

• Cut an additional strip 6" wide across the sheet, which you can cut into eight 6" x 6" pieces. These will support the top of the launcher.

2. Glue and nail the eight supports onto the base at each corner. Then flip the assembly upside down and repeat the process to attach the top. Let the glue dry completely.

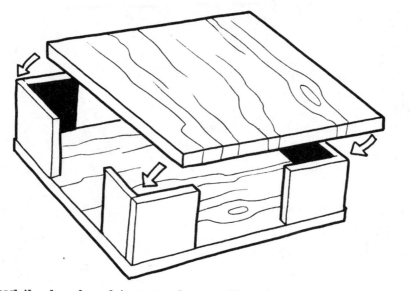

3. While the glue dries, cut the steel bar into three pieces: two that are a foot long each, and one that is 3" long. If you don't have a saw to cut metal, see if your hardware store can cut it for you. Drill a $1/4$" hole one inch from one end of the two longer pieces, and another hole 3" from the other end of each piece. Then drill a hole in the middle of the shorter piece.

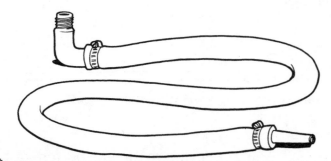

4. Secure one end of the rubber hose to the PVC elbow with a hose clamp.
• Jam the tire valve stem into the other end of the hose and secure it with the other hose clamp.

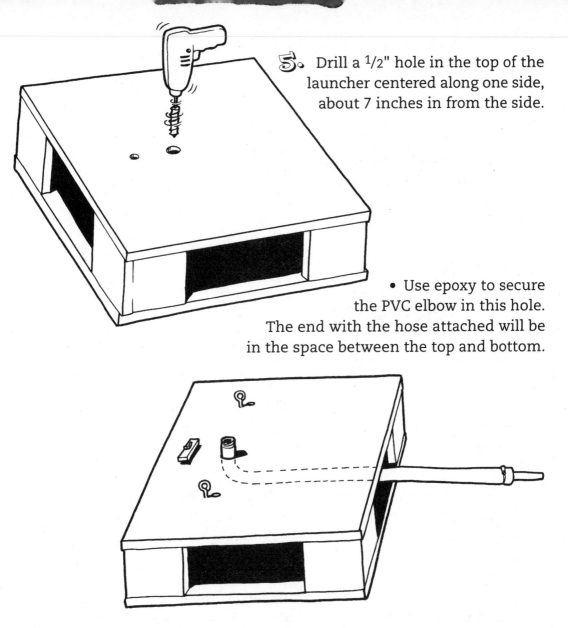

5. Drill a 1/2" hole in the top of the launcher centered along one side, about 7 inches in from the side.

• Use epoxy to secure the PVC elbow in this hole. The end with the hose attached will be in the space between the top and bottom.

6. Drill a 1/4" hole through the top 3" from the protruding PVC elbow.

• This hole should be along the center line (as is the hole for the PVC) and about half way between the PVC hole and the edge of the top.

• Run a bolt up from underneath through this hole, drop a spring on top, then the 3" piece of steel bar, and secure it with a wing nut.

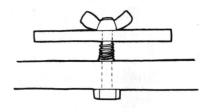

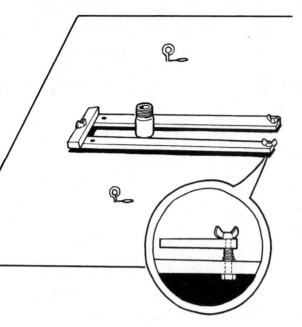

7. Drill two starter holes first, and then attach two screw eyes to the top of the launcher, on either side of, and in line with the PVC elbow. Locate these 7" from the outer edges of the top.

8. Line up the two long steel bars on the top, parallel to each other so one end of each is covered by the shorter steel bar.

• Drill holes to secure the opposite ends with bolts. The holes should be about 1¼" apart along the center line.

• Push the bolt up from underneath and drop a spring on it.

• Put one of the steel bars on the bolt and hold it in place with a wing nut.

• Repeat for the second bar.

9. Drill a starter hole and then secure the remaining screw eye in the center of the dowel so it can be a handle.

10. Assemble the release mechanism.

• Tie one end of the rope to a steel bar and lead the rope through the screw eye on the same side of the top of the launcher.

• Lead the rope through the screw eye on the handle and through the screw eye on the other side of the top.

• Tie it off on the other steel bar.

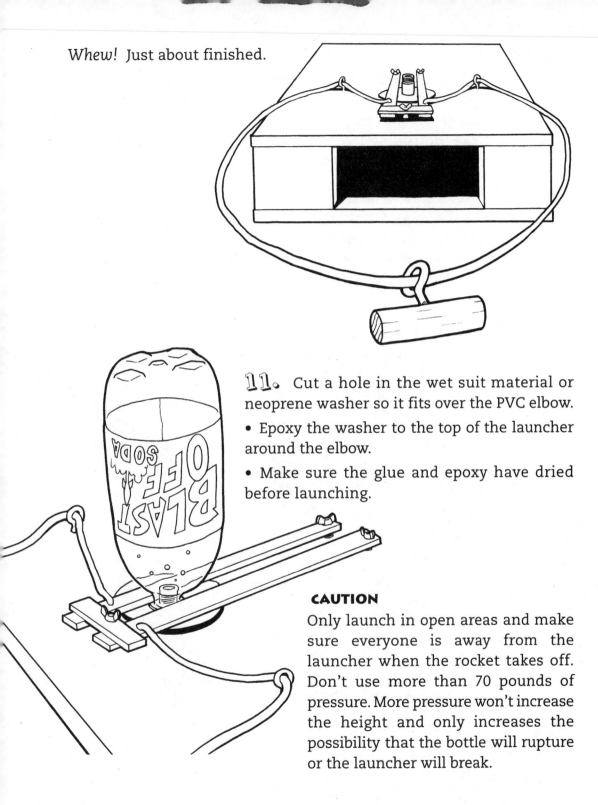

Whew! Just about finished.

11. Cut a hole in the wet suit material or neoprene washer so it fits over the PVC elbow.

• Epoxy the washer to the top of the launcher around the elbow.

• Make sure the glue and epoxy have dried before launching.

CAUTION

Only launch in open areas and make sure everyone is away from the launcher when the rocket takes off. Don't use more than 70 pounds of pressure. More pressure won't increase the height and only increases the possibility that the bottle will rupture or the launcher will break.

LAUNCHING

If you haven't seen a bottle rocket launcher in action, you will be surprised. Set it up in an open area and expect the bottle to reach 100 feet. Add a few inches of water to a 2-liter bottle, and invert the bottle over the protruding PVC pipe. Press the bottle hard against the neoprene washer to prevent water from leaking out.

Use the two steel bars to hold the bottle in place by clamping them over the lip on the neck of the bottle. Pinch the two bars together with one hand and tighten the wing nut holding the short steel bar with the other hand. When the bars are tight enough to stay in place when you release your grip, you're ready to pressurize the bottle.

Attach the bike pump to the valve stem and start pumping. For the first few launches, keep the pressure under 40 pounds per square inch. When the bottle has been pressurized, sit on the ground with your feet against the side of the launcher. Put on the safety goggles and have everyone else stand at least ten feet back. Make sure the rope can run freely through all the screw eyes. You don't want the rope to pull one of the steel bars before the other. Pull on the handle to yank the two steel bars back. You will get wet as the rocket blasts off.

RESULTS Awesome! You can launch a bottle rocket 100 feet or more.

WHAT'S HAPPENING?

The pressure inside the bottle forces the water and air out the opening, which propels the bottle in the opposite direction.

FANTASTIC FLYING FACTS

At the 1996 California State Championship for Science Olympiad, one bottle rocket entry, equipped with a parachute, remained in the air for over twenty minutes. The wind caught it and held it aloft until the judges couldn't see it.

Spuds in space

OVERVIEW Launch potato parts with a safe rocket launcher to appreciate the power of compressed air.

MATERIALS
- electrical conduit — EMT, 3/4" diameter and 4' long (available in hardware stores)
- 4' long dowel that barely slides inside the EMT
- bag of spuds

CONSTRUCTION

1. Hold a spud on top of the conduit and whack on it a few times with the palm of your hand. You will jam a cylinder of potato into the opening.

- When the conduit has cut through the potato, pull the rest of the spud up and off the conduit. You will be left with a plug of spud in the conduit.

- Repeat the procedure on the other end. Now it's fully loaded.

LAUNCHING

Force the dowel into one end of the conduit a few inches. Place the other end of the dowel on the ground. Keeping your feet clear of the dowel, pull the conduit down toward the ground to launch your spud ship skyward.

RESULTS

You can launch a spud core across your yard and hear a satisfying "plumph" sound.

PLUMPH!

POTATOES   CARROTS   LETTUCE   CORN

WHAT'S HAPPENING?

The spud plugs act as gaskets to trap the air inside the conduit. When you force the lower one upward by pulling the conduit down, you compress the air, increasing the air pressure inside the conduit. The pressure increases until it explodes the spud out the top of the launcher.

What else?

◎ You might try other sizes of conduit to see if you can get longer flights. Or, you might try other fruits or vegetables. Can you find a substitute for spuds?

SCIENCE FAIR

A simple experiment you could conduct in a field or large yard would be to see what launch angle gives the longest flights.

• You would need to build a launch tower to hold the conduit at the desired angle, from nearly parallel to the ground to pointing straight up.

• Also, you would want to launch several times at each angle to average the flight distances which are bound to vary from one launch to the next.

Riding hovercraft 19

OVERVIEW Ride a hovercraft you can build.

MATERIALS
- $1/2$ sheet of $3/8$" plywood, any grade
- plastic sheeting – at least 5' x 5', 4 mil or thicker (10 mil is best)
- duct tape
- drill and bits
- coffee can lid, or circle of wood of the same size
- nut and bolt to fit through the lid
- 2 washers
- hole saw
- scissors
- powerful leaf blower or shop vac with blower

CONSTRUCTION

1. Find the center of the 5' x 5' piece of plywood and draw the largest complete circle using a string and pencil.

- Have an adult cut out the circle.

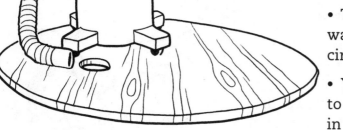

2. Place the leaf blower or shop vac on the circle and decide where it can sit while blowing air through a hole in the plywood.

- The hole should be about half way between the center of the circle and the outer edge.
- You can use duct tape later to secure the hose or nozzle in place.

3. Drill a hole through the center of the plywood and through the coffee can lid or its wooden substitute.

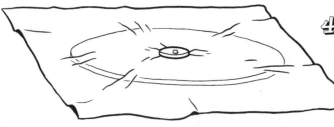

4. Center the plastic sheeting over the plywood and lay the lid on top of the plastic.

- Push the bolt through the washer, lid, plastic, plywood and second washer, and bolt it securely.
- Now attach the sides of the plastic.

5. Flip the plywood and plastic sheet upside down so you can tape the plastic to the top of the wood.

- Start at the middle of one edge and tape the plastic so it has a couple of inches of belly on the underside.

• Continue taping around the circle, trying to keep about the same amount of loose plastic on the underside.

6. Flip the hovercraft over. Using a 2" lid from a jar as a guide, cut four circles out of the plastic on the underside.

• Space these evenly around the circle, a little more than half way from the center to the edge.

LAUNCHING

This hovercraft will slide across a smooth floor, like smooth tile. Place the nozzle or hose of the blower into the hole, and tape it in place. Turn on the blower. The plastic will inflate with air, raising the hovercraft off the ground. Check for leaks and secure them with duct tape. When you're satisfied that it's holding air well, turn off the blower.

With the blower off, sit on the hovercraft just behind the center of the circle with your feet wrapped up in front of you. Turn on the blower. If the bag doesn't inflate and lift you off the floor, have someone raise one side to help the air fill the plastic. Reposition yourself so you're in the center. Once the plastic is inflated, have someone give you a gentle push or spin.

RESULTS
You can slide across a smooth floor.

WHAT'S HAPPENING?
The inflated bag is spreading your weight over a large area reducing the pressure (your weight and the weight of the hovercraft divided by the area of plastic touching the floor and supporting your weight). Air escaping from underneath the hovercraft reduces the friction further and you are able to slide easily.

What else?
◎ Figure out a way to propel yourself while sitting on your hovercraft.

Experimental flyer 20

OVERVIEW This paper airplane demonstrates how planes turn.

MATERIALS
- 8 1/2" x 11" sheet of paper
- scissors
- paper clip

CONSTRUCTION

This plane is the common dart with a few extra features.

- Fold the paper in half, lengthwise, and unfold it.
- Pull one corner to the centerline so the top edge of the paper aligns on the centerfold. Then give it a firm smooth crease.
- Repeat for the other corner.
- Repeat this process twice more on each side.
- Fold the two wings away from each other along the centerline. Make a firm crease on the center line and put a paper clip to hold the folds together.

LAUNCHING

Grab the dart near its center of gravity, its *balance point*. Pull your arm back and fling it. With neat folds and solid creases, your plane should fly straight and far.

Modification 1

Up to this point the plane is a dart. Now you're ready to transform it into an experimental plane. With scissors, make a cut on each side of the back of the wing about 1¼" in from the sides. Make the cut 1" long, parallel to the outside edge.

TEST PILOT 1

You've just made flaps on the wings of your plane. Bend them up slightly and relaunch. The plane will rise and travel slower. By raising the "elevator" you added drag to the plane and depressed the tail. As you launched it, the nose went up.

If you use a large angle on the elevator the plane will rise, stall, and fall to the ground. Airplanes have stall warning devices to tell the pilots they are climbing too steeply for their speed and are getting close to stalling the plane.

What happens when you depress the elevators down?

Try one flap up slightly and one down slightly. The plane will spiral in flight. Now, let's make another modification to make the plane turn.

Modification 2

Make a rudder for the plane. Cut 1" in on the vertical part of the tail, about 1" from the bottom. Make the cut parallel to the bottom of the plane.

TEST PILOT 2

Bend the flaps or elevators back to the neutral position
and bend the rudder to one side.
Try flying the plane.

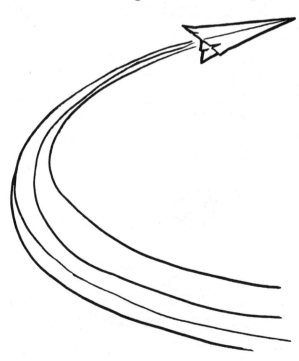

TEST PILOT 3

To turn your plane, copy Glenn Curtiss: push the rudder to the right, raise the left flap slightly and lower the right flap slightly. With a gentle launch, the plane will turn to the right. This is how planes turn.

WHAT'S HAPPENING?

To make a turn while riding a bike, you turn the wheel and lean into the turn. If you're traveling fast and you don't lean as you turn, you'll fall. Planes have the same problem. To solve the problem planes have *ailerons*, flaps that assist turning by banking the plane, and a rudder to turn it.

What else?

◎ Try different combinations of flaps and rudder
to see which gives graceful turns.

FANTASTIC FLYING FACTS

Early aviators tried to make turns by using a rudder only,
and they had the same success your plane did.
The Wright Brothers figured out how to bend wings and turn the rudder
at the same time and that let them be the first to fly.
Glenn Curtiss and Alexander Graham Bell improved their design
by inventing flaps on the end of the wings, called ailerons.